A special gift for you,

the new mother

 Presented to

With love from

© 2015 Ta-Ha Publishers Ltd
First Published in April 2016
by
Ta-Ha Publishers Ltd,
Unit 4, The Windsor Centre,
Windsor Grove, West Norwood,
London, SE27 9NT, UK
www.tahapublishers.com

Written by: Muneeba Zahid
Edited by: Amna Ahmad MBBS and Abia Afsar-Siddiqui PhD
Cover and book design by: Shakir Abdulcadir > opensquares.uk
Printed and bound by: IMAK Ofset, Turkey

A catalogue record of this book is available from the British Library
ISBN: 978 1 84200 159 2

The information in this book does not intend to be a substitute for qualified medical advice. The points raised and suggestions made are from the author's own perspective and experience. Always consult with a medical practitioner about any health or well-being concerns. Neither the author nor the publisher can be held responsible for any claim or loss arising out of the use or misuse of the suggestions made. Failure to seek medical advice is upon the individual.

A Gift for the New
Muslim Mother

Muneeba
Zahid

TA–HA Publishers Ltd

Contents

For my beautiful little
Rukayya, Ismael and Aamina,
whom Allah has blessed me with;
and to my family.

Why I wrote the book...

As a new mother, I felt the need for guidance from an Islamic perspective. With the ups and downs, hormonal changes and new responsibilities ahead of me, I felt quite overwhelmed. I yearned to reconnect with Islam to help me focus on my new role as a mother more effectively, but I didn't feel I had the time to sit and read through long volumes. I hope that this small book helps fill that empty void that the new mother may feel, which I initially felt too.

Muneeba
x

Amazing
Motherhood

*N*othing can compare to what a mother feels and can do for her child. Right from the moment that you found out you were expecting, Allah filled your heart with an abundance of love and mercy. And when your baby was born, she too looked at you with adoring eyes and complete trust.

Allah has placed in your hands the trust and privilege of raising your child to be pious and righteous, to walk on the straight path of Islam. You will be the first school for your child, passing on your knowledge, mannerisms, behaviour and routines to the next generation of Muslims.

You will hold their hand on this unique and joyous journey that is motherhood. Along that journey there will be a whole spectrum of emotions, new responsibilities and sometimes overwhelming concerns. It is so easy to get caught up in the daily grind.

When you feel that your life consists of nothing more than dirty nappies and wet bibs, sleepless nights and constant demands on your time, then always remember the following hadith which beautifully outlines the rewards for your struggle:

Salamah, the wet nurse of Ibrahim, the son of the Prophet ﷺ, said, *"O Messenger of Allah. You give tidings of all the good to the men and you don't give tidings to the women." He said, "Did your female companions induce you to [ask] this?" She said, "Yes." He said, "Will one of you not be pleased that when she is pregnant from her husband and he is pleased with her that she has a reward like the reward of the one who fasts and prays in the way of Allah? Then when she is in labour, none of the people of the heavens or the earth know what is hidden for her of [pleasures] soothing to her eyes. And when she delivers, no mouthful of milk flows from her nor a [child's] suck except that she has a reward with every mouthful and with every suck. And if [her child] keeps her awake during the night, she has a reward similar to the reward of freeing seventy slaves for the sake of Allah."* (Sunan Ibn Majah)

But you must never lose sight of the bigger picture: children are a joy to have and raise. They are the youth of tomorrow upon whom the call to Islam falls and are an adornment for this world. They are an asset to their parents in this life and the Hereafter, as another hadith explains:

And the Messenger of Allah ﷺ said, *"A man will be raised in status in Paradise and will say, 'Where did this come from?' And it will be said, 'From your son's praying for forgiveness for you.'"* (Sunan Ibn Majah)

You are able to bring stability to your little one's life, along with Islamic knowledge, love, comfort and warmth, insha'Allah. These qualities will influence your baby positively and, in turn, help to create a better society. Bringing up righteous children who worship Allah alone is the most rewarding achievement a parent can be proud of.

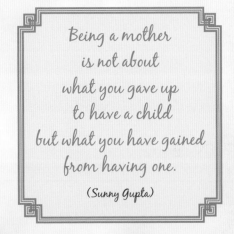

Being a mother
is not about
what you gave up
to have a child
but what you have gained
from having one.

(Sunny Gupta)

Becoming
A Mother

*N*o one can really explain to you how much your life will change after having a baby. You may now start to feel that getting through the long nine months of pregnancy and difficult labour was, in hindsight, the easy part. Now motherhood dawns upon you with all its rewards and challenges.

With a quiet little sleeping baby next to you, you know that now your life has taken a major turning point and that change lies ahead. Your life will now be dedicated to taking care of this new little being Allah has gifted to you.

As everything starts becoming less blurry, reality starts to kick in. With many sleepless nights ahead, feeding and changing, soothing your baby to sleep after she threw up all over you in the middle of the night, you know that you are in for the long haul!

You will learn and discover so much about yourself and your baby as you embark on this beautiful journey. The first few days and weeks may well leave you shell-shocked and seem never-ending but everything will start to slowly settle down.

There are three major main points to bear in mind at this stage:

❖ No doubt people will give you advice and you will read books on the subject, but at the end of the day, trust your maternal instinct to do what is right for your child and given your circumstances.

❖ Putting your baby into some sort of routine could be a good idea for both of you. Babies usually thrive on having a routine as they know what to expect and when to expect it, for example, napping, waking, bathing and feeding. However, do not be too hard on yourself if establishing a routine takes time. You are both learning to adjust to a new life.

❖ Don't forget to enjoy each stage of parenting! When every day seems to blend into another one full of endless chores, then take five minutes to stop and think about the bigger picture. We have been trusted by Allah to take care of the greatest asset on earth – a little person full of love, hope and innocence.

There are so many things for you to look forward to with your little one. Their first step, their first word… it may seem like a long way to go but time will whizz past and before you know it, they will be starting nursery.

TOP TIP
Buy a baby keepsake book
so that you can write
all of those things your baby did
for the first time -
a lovely way to look back
and cherish their childhood.

Welcoming
Your Newborn
In Islam

*T*here are a few beautiful *sunnah*s that are recommended to be carried out following the birth of the baby. Far from being empty rituals, they safeguard the physical and spiritual well-being of the baby as well as being a time for sharing your joy with family, friends and the poor alike.

The following two *sunnah*s should be performed as soon as possible following the birth of the baby:

1) RECITING THE ADHAN
2) TAHNEEK

1) Reciting the Adhan

Unfortunately, even a newborn is under attack from Shaytan (Satan) from the moment it is born. This is why it cries at birth due to Shaytan never leaving his enemy without harming it.

The Prophet ﷺ said, *"When any human being is born, Satan pinches the body with his two fingers, except Isa ﷺ, the son of Maryam, whom Satan tried to pinch but failed, for he touched the placenta cover instead."* (Sahih al-Bukhari)

It is mentioned in a hadith that the Shaytan runs away at the sound of the *adhan*, and so the *adhan* should be recited in the right ear of the baby by a pious Muslim male elder as soon as possible after the birth. Doing so will also ensure that the very first words that a baby hears are those confirming the Oneness and Greatness of Allah.

Abu Raf'i relates that, *"I saw the Prophet ﷺ saying the adhan of salah in the ear of his grandson, Hasan, when the child was born to his daughter Fatimah."* (Musnad Ahmad)

2) Tahneek

During the time of the Prophet ﷺ, when a newborn was given to him, he would chew the pulp of a date and apply it to the baby's palate with his finger. He would follow this by rubbing its chin to train it to eat. This was performed so that the child would be kept safe from evil.

Aisha narrates that, *"The people used to bring their newborn children to the Prophet ﷺ and he would bless them and perform the tahneek."* (Sahih Muslim)

The Prophet ﷺ chewed the date because his saliva was blessed by Allah. However, it is not essential to chew the date before putting it in the baby's mouth; it can be softened between the fingers. This *sunnah* can be performed by the father, the mother or a pious Muslim whose supplication is hope to be accepted by Allah, again as soon as possible after the birth.

The following three *sunnah*s are preferably carried out on the seventh day after the birth of the baby according to the following hadith:

Every child is held in pledge for its aqeeqah, which is sacrificed for him on his seventh day and he is named on it and his head is shaved. (Musnad Ahmad and Sunan Abu Dawud)

3) Aqeeqah

It is a *sunnah* to sacrifice an animal in celebration of the birth of a baby, preferably on the seventh day after birth. Whilst sacrificing the animal, it is obligatory to mention the name of Allah and it is advised to mention the name of the child. It is recommended to sacrifice one animal for a girl and two animals for a boy, with the meat to be distributed to family, friends and the poor. Cooking the meat prior to distribution leads to greater blessing.

4) Shaving the head hair

It is recommended to shave the head hair of the baby following the sacrifice. The hair should then be weighed and the value of the equivalent weight of silver should be given to the poor.

When Hasan was born, he ﷺ said to her (Fatima), *"Shave his head and give the weight of his hair in silver to the poor."* (Musnad Ahmad and Sunan al-Bayhaqi)

5) Tasmiyyah

It is a *sunnah* for the baby, as well as their right, to be given a good and meaningful name. The Prophet ﷺ used to ensure that if a name was given to someone, it should have a beautiful meaning and if it did not, then he would change to it something else that was more appropriate.

Additionally, in the case of a baby boy:

6) Khitan

The circumcision is an important practice for a newborn baby boy. It was practised by Prophet Ibrahim عليه السلام and continued through to the Prophet Muhammad ﷺ. It is recommended to take place on the seventh day but there is no sin if it is delayed. In any case, it should be carried out before the child reaches puberty. A medical practitioner trained in this area should perform this procedure to minimise any complications. And finally...

7) Announcing the birth

Announcing the arrival of your new bundle of joy is one of the most exciting parts of parenthood. The joy and happiness everyone feels is a cause for celebration, thanks to Allah and *du'a*s for the newborn.

The following *du'a* is recommended to be supplicated for the new parents:

بَارَكَ اللَّهُ لَكَ فِي الْمَوْهُوبِ لَكَ وَشَكَرْتَ الْوَاهِبَ وَبَلَغَ أَشُدَّهُ وَرُزِقْتَ بِرَّهُ

Barakallahu laka fil-mawhoobi laka, wa shakartal-wahiba, wa balagha 'ashuddahu, wa ruziqta birrahu

May Allah bless you with His gift to you, and may you (the new parent) give thanks, may the child reach the maturity of years, and may you be granted its righteousness.

And the parents should respond with:

بَارَكَ اللَّهُ لَكَ وَبَارَكَ عَلَيْكَ وَجَزَاكَ اللَّهُ خَيْرًا أَوْ رَزَقَكَ اللَّهُ مِثْلَهُ وَأَجْزَلَ ثَوَابَكَ

Barakallahu laka wa baaraka 'alayka, wa jazakallahu khayran, wa razaqakallahu mithlahu, wa ajzala thawabaka

May Allah bless you, and shower His blessings upon you, and may Allah reward you well and bestow upon you its like and reward you abundantly.[1]

---

1 An-Nawawi, Kitabul-'Athkar

Breastfeeding

*F*eeding your little newborn has to be one of the most important aspects of motherhood. Healthcare professionals recommend breastfeeding exclusively for the first six months of a baby's life. Islamically, you can breastfeed an infant up to two years of age. Breast milk is the most nutritious, complete and tailor made meal that a baby can have. Not only can it reduce the incidence of some medical issues in later life for the baby but also for the mother. On an emotional level, it promotes the special bond of closeness between mother and child.

For many mothers and babies, the process of breastfeeding is relatively straightforward with the mother producing an adequate quantity of milk for her child and the baby able to latch on and feed without problems.

However, sometimes it can be a bumpy ride getting your baby to drink milk let alone breastfeed. Some babies are not able to latch on effectively and suck strongly; the mother's milk supply may not be adequate or the baby may have been born prematurely or needing special care. Whatever the reason, it can be an emotional time for a mother if she struggles to breastfeed. You may feel frustrated with yourself, overwhelmed by advice that may conflict with your instincts, concerned about the effects of topping up with formula milk on your own milk production. This is entirely natural.

If you are having a hard time breastfeeding, then it is very important that you seek specialist help at the start. The sooner you seek help, the easier it is to resolve. Organisations such as La Leche League or the National Childbirth Trust have trained, volunteer breastfeeding counsellors that can guide and support you. If you need more intensive help, you can hire an IBCLC (International Board Certified Lactation Consultant) to assist you through this period.

In the end, it really boils down to how your birth went and how well you and your baby are after birth which can subsequently lead to a "better" breast feeder or not. No two babies are the same so try not to compare yourself (or allow yourself to be compared) to another mother.

TOP TIP

Ensure that you are getting
nutritious, regular meals;
drinking plenty of water
and getting rest.

Your Health

Motherhood brings with it many trials and tribulations as well as numerous and unexpected joys and pleasures. Your body and mind have been through an enormous number of changes through the nine months of pregnancy and in the aftermath of the birth. Of course, it is normal to feel physically, emotionally and spiritually drained. At every stage of motherhood, you will face new challenges: changing sleep routines, weaning, teething, teaching them speech, potty training and so on. Therefore, it is very important that you do not neglect yourself and your well-being in the early stages of this wonderful journey.

Physical Changes

Physically you may be feeling all sorts of aches and pains such as:

- Pain with your uterus contracting especially during breastfeeding
- Stitches
- Caesarean delivery wound pain
- Haemorrhoid irritation
- Back pain
- Soreness in breasts and nipples

For a mum-to-be all of these issues may sound quite unappetising but insha'Allah most of these will get better with time and self-care. Listen to your body and allow it to rest and recover. In the meantime, remember that a believer's sins are expiated for even the prick of a thorn (Sahih al-Bukhari and Muslim), so the aches you experience after giving birth are all a source of reward.

Top Tip
Use rosehip oil to help soothe away those stretch marks post birth. Also, sitting in a warm bath with a couple of drops of tea tree oil can help speed up the healing of your perineal area.

Your body needs time to heal and adjust to the dramatic changes and will respond well to rest and a nutritious diet. However, if an issue does not subside and you are concerned about it, always seek medical advice.

A very effective *du'a* that you can recite when feeling physical discomfort, whilst placing your hand on the affected area, is:

بِسْمِ اللهِ

Bismillah (3 times)

followed by

أَعُوذُ بِاللهِ وَقُدْرَتِهِ مِن شَرِّ مَا أَجِدُ وَأُحَاذِرُ

A'oodhu bi'izzatil-lahi waqudratihi min sharri ma ajidu wa uhadhir
(7 times)

In the name of Allah.
I seek refuge in the Exalted Power and Glory of Allah from which I feel and fear.[2]

Emotional Changes

Most new mothers experience a variety of emotions, particularly in the first few weeks after giving birth. You have just been through one of the biggest life changes possible, hormones are rushing around inside you, and you are taking care of a baby while sacrificing your own sleep and needs. No wonder you sometimes have moments when you start questioning yourself, having self-doubts and wondering whether you can make it to the end of the day!

2 Sahih Muslim

The first thing you can do is trust in Allah. That means really believing in Him, His mercy and in the abilities He has gifted you with to get you through this turbulent period. Allah has said in the Qur'an:

"Allah does not burden a soul more than it can bear."
(Surah 2:284)

Motherhood is a steep learning curve. Day by day you will instinctively understand what your child needs and settle into your role as the best mother to your child.

The other important thing is to have a support network. A close friend whom you can phone and have a cry to; family members that will take over parenting and household duties when you need a break; a circle of local new mums that you can share this journey with; healthcare professionals that you can discuss your health needs with. This team of people will quite literally carry you through the days when you feel that you can't do it alone, so rely on them and they will be only too glad to help.

TOP TIP

Give your baby massages. This is a wonderful way of connecting with him/her. They will also really enjoy it too.

There will of course be days when everything gets to you and you just want to have a good cry. That's fine. Go ahead and get it out of your system. But when you have finished, spare a moment to count your blessings, too. You'll always find something to smile about through your tears. The Prophet Muhammad ﷺ said:

"Look at those who are below you, not at those who are above you, so that you will not think little of the blessings that Allah has bestowed upon you." (Musnad Ahmad)

Baby Blues or Post-Natal Depression?

Even though having a baby is a happy life event, it is natural to feel a bit down in the dumps after childbirth. Most women experience the 'baby blues' within a few days of giving birth and the symptoms include:

- Feeling low
- Feeling anxious
- Feeling irritable and more sensitive than usual
- Have mood swings
- Feeling weepy for no reason

These feelings usually reach their worst on the fourth or fifth day after your baby is born. They may last for a few hours or a few days, but they usually go away by the tenth day after the birth. You may feel alone and like you are the only one feeling these feelings. Talking to family, friends and your healthcare professional are all ways of helping you get through this hard stage.

Whilst baby blues are quite common and do eventually subside, postnatal depression is more serious and should be tackled as soon as the symptoms start to surface. According to the NHS website, it affects one in ten women usually beginning within the first six months of giving birth. However, it can occur at any time within the first year.

You may be experiencing postnatal depression if you find that your symptoms are affecting your quality of life and include:

- Feeling overwhelmed and unable to cope
- Crying all the time
- Feeling uninterested in the baby
- Sleeplessness and loss of appetite
- Anxiety and panic attacks

If you are experiencing any of these symptoms or even if you are just unsure, it is important to contact a healthcare professional. PND is a medical condition and not at all a reflection of you or your parenting abilities.

Taking
Care
of Yourself

The laundry is piling up, the dishes are taking over the kitchen and yet you don't seem to get a moment's break day or night, every single day. You can't carry on like this and besides, every mum deserves pampering and the time to put her feet up and just...be.

Taking care of yourself and wanting some time away from routine is not selfish or unreasonable and it shouldn't be a luxury. In fact, it is an important part of your duties, otherwise you will end up being of no use to anyone.

Schedule some time every week when someone trusted can look after the baby and use that time for YOU – not the dishes or the laundry – and do whatever you want to do that will help you de-stress and unwind. You might like to:

- Lie back in a warm relaxing bath
- Enjoy a spa treatment or massage
- Go out with your husband or friends
- Read a book with your feet up and savour a mug of your favourite hot drink

Even if you have a regular slot of dedicated "me-time", that doesn't mean that you can neglect yourself at other times. Taking care of yourself in small ways each and every day will keep you in the best of physical and emotional health. These include:

- Making sure that you drink plenty of water
- Ensure that you are eating nutritious regular meals and have a multivitamin supplement if your healthcare professional recommends
- Getting out every day even if it is for a ten minute walk down the road. Fresh air is so good for clearing the mind
- Joining a mother and baby exercise class or a group buggy walking session will help keep stress levels under control. If that is not possible, then at least try to follow an exercise routine at home with a DVD
- Attending a mother and baby group locally to share your experiences and build back your social life
- Napping when your baby naps

These suggestions will insha'Allah help you to stay, not only in good physical health, but also boost your self-esteem and social life, which can both take a bruising in the weeks and months after birth. It can sometimes be a struggle to rediscover your identity now that your primary role in life has changed as has your daily routine. However, building up a new and varied routine will help you settle into the new role more seamlessly.

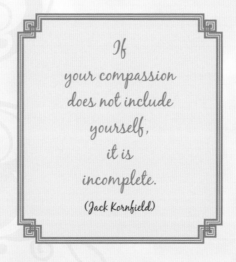

If your compassion does not include yourself, it is incomplete.

(Jack Kornfield)

Managing
Your Time

*W*e all know that babies take up a lot of time! That is not necessarily a bad thing but you may feel like you are unable to get your jobs done because of the demands of motherhood. You may even feel like you do not have enough time to concentrate on *ibadah*. This is why time management is quite a useful skill to have if you wish to gain control of where your time is going and how you can manage your day better. Ideally, you should be able to find time within the day to:

- Spend plenty of quality bonding time with your baby
- Have some time for self-care as we discussed earlier
- Manage the household chores
- Fit in all the healthcare appointments that are scheduled for you and the baby

If that is proving difficult more often than not, then it may be worth asking yourself three key questions that will help you to manage your time more effectively:

1) Where is my time going?
2) What would I like to achieve?
3) How am I going to achieve my goals?

1) Where Is My Time Going?

To start with, spend ten minutes before you go to sleep, jotting down exactly what you did, if possible, in hourly chunks. Do this over the course of a week and you will easily be able to see where your time is going, when you are more productive, when your baby sleeps and feeds etc.

Unfortunately we can all waste a little bit of time here and there such as spending too much time browsing the internet, watching television or on the phone. Suddenly the time whizzes past and before you know it it's time to go to bed before having achieved much in your day. You go to bed with that nagging feeling that the day was not fulfilling, but we all wake up the next day and do the same thing over again!

Value your time like gold. More experienced mums will tell you that these early days are very precious and it is worth making a conscious effort to get the most out of them.

I would suggest you begin by reducing and/or eliminating

activities that are not beneficial to you and the goals you want to achieve. This makes space for things which we all complain that we never have any time for!

Next turn your attention to the chores that need to be done in order to run the house but aren't always enjoyable. Think about how these could be delegated or streamlined to get them done in less time. Would it help to invest in a dishwasher, hire a cleaner or make use of a local ironing service? It is not a priority for the house to be immaculate these days or gourmet meals to be served up twice a day. Can you use some shortcuts in your cooking, prepare meals ahead of time, share out the most time consuming jobs with other members of the family?

Now that you have de-cluttered your day and "made" more time, you can now think about how you would like to make better use of it.

TOP TIP

Arrange your baby's clothes in order of age.

0-3 months in one box,

3-6 months in another

and so on.

This will help you use all your baby's clothes more efficiently.

2) What Would I Like To Achieve?

There are two types of activities in life:

1. The things we have to do in order to fulfil our basic needs and achieve a decent standard of existence for ourselves and our family. These are things like domestic chores and earning a living.
2. The things we would like to do in order to realise our best selves and achieve a high quality of life. These are things that add to our emotional well-being, strengthen social interactions and enhance our spirituality.

The key to a contented life is to strike a balance between the two. We all tend to spend too much time on the mundane chores but not enough time on the things that give our life meaning. Think about which areas of your life may be getting neglected and then list specific and realistic aims to restore balance. Imagine you had a twenty-fifth hour in the day, what would you choose to do with it?

For example, if your goals are to get closer to Allah, put more effort in your marriage and gain more confidence by losing the baby weight, then your aims might look something like this:

a) Perform *tahajjud* salah when I wake up for the night feed

b) Spend half an hour uninterrupted and device-free time every evening with my husband

c) Join the mother and baby buggy walk in the local park on Thursday morning

3) How Can I Achieve It?

Making lists is one of the most effective tools to use in time management. It helps you to see clearly what needs to be done and when and saves you holding everything in your head. Use a diary, family organiser or calendar to make your list that is always prominently displayed where the family can see it. You can set up reminder alarms on your mobile phone for important appointments.

Prioritise your daily or weekly activities into one of the following categories:

1) Urgent and important
2) Important but not urgent
3) Urgent but not as important
4) Not urgent or as important

If you get the urgent and important stuff out of the way first, it leaves you more relaxed to enjoy your day rather than being frazzled at the end of it.

Time management is the key to helping you achieve the things you want within a suitable and realistic time frame. It will make you feel in control of your life and far more contented in the long term.

The life of this world is made up of three days: yesterday has gone with all that was done; tomorrow you may never reach but today is for you, so do what you should do today.

(Hasan al-Basri)

Creating an Islamic Home

Creating an Islamic environment at home is one of the most precious gifts you can give your family. It helps your child to establish an Islamic identity and a connection with Allah from an early age. The beauty of Islam is that it is a natural part of everything we do. *Ibadah* is not just praying and reciting the Qur'an. Feeding, changing and playing with your child with the intention of pleasing Allah is *ibadah*, as is cooking for your family and cleaning. Let your child see the natural connection with Allah in everything we do in our lives.

Involving your baby in acts of worship will also help establish the foundations of an Islamic home.

This beautifully illustrates the kind nature parents should show towards their children at all times.

Young children imitate and mirror what they are exposed to from an early age. This is all a part of their learning process which is why as mothers, we need to display good actions, qualities, mannerisms and behaviour so that our children can follow. After all, home is the very first school that our children attend and we are their very first teachers and role models.

Children gain an understanding and absorb information from their environment through first-hand experiences and this stays with them far more solidly than anything they are told to do. So if your baby can visualise you (and the rest of the family members) performing *salah* regularly, engaging in *dhikr*, reading the Qur'an, always smiling and being helpful and kind to others, then this, insha'Allah, will set the foundation for their future lives and allow to them to connect deeply with Islam.

TOP TIP

Play a Qur'an recitation
on low volume
in your baby's room
for a little while every day.
Their little hearts and
minds will become
accustomed
to the words of Allah
from a young age.

With the little bundle in your arms, comes a huge responsibility. Not only must you care for your baby physically, mentally and emotionally, but also pass on to them the teachings of Islam and instil in them the noble character of the Prophet Muhammad ﷺ. That responsibility begins from the day that they are born.

Abdullah ibn Umar reported: The Messenger of Allah ﷺ said, *"Every one of you is a shepherd and is responsible for his flock. The leader of people is a guardian and is responsible for his subjects. A man is the guardian of his family and he is responsible for them. A woman is the guardian of her husband's home and his children and she is responsible for them. The servant of a man is a guardian of the property of his master and he is responsible for it. Surely, every one of you is a shepherd and responsible for his flock."* (Sahih al-Bukhari and Muslim)

Connecting
With the Creator

After having a baby, it may be difficult to reconnect yourself with your *deen* due to your new responsibility, the post natal bleeding[3] you are experiencing and the hormonal changes you are going through. However, it is ultimately the connection with Allah that will help you to get through the rough times so it is worth nurturing this.

Dhikr

Dhikr, the remembrance of Allah, is an excellent means of affirming your belief in Allah and increasing your faith. Its importance is paramount and extremely beneficial as stated in the Quran.

"O ye who believe! Celebrate the praises of Allah and do this often; and glorify Him morning and evening. He it is Who sends blessings on you, as do His angels, that He may bring you out from the depths of darkness into light..." (Surah 33:41–43)

---

3 *Nifas*, or post-natal bleeding, is the period of bleeding following childbirth in which a woman is excused from performing *salah*, fasting and touching a *mushaf* (copy of the Qur'an). The maximum period of *nifas* is forty days after which it is compulsory to perform *ghusl* and resume the above religious duties.

During your post natal bleeding period, you can keep your heart alive through good deeds and engaging your tongue with the remembrance and praise of Allah. Some suggestions that I have found helpful are:

❖ Repeating the *Shahada* affirms your faith and keeps you focussed on what the whole point of our existence is.

❖ *The Prophet ﷺ said: "The most beloved words to Allah are four:* **SubhanAllah** - *Glorified is Allah, and* **Walhamdulillah** - *The Praise is for Allah, and* **Wa la ilaha ill Allah** - *There is none worthy of worship but Allah, and* **Wallahu Akbar** - *Allah is the Most Great."* (Sahih Muslim)

❖ Reciting some or all of the ninety-nine names of Allah can bring you closer to Allah and thinking about His attributes can be quite amazing and awe-inspiring when we are caught up in our own problems. It is stated in the Qur'an:

"Allah has the Most Beautiful Names; so call Him by them." (Surah 7:180)

❖ Recite short recommended *surahs* at specific times of the day and they soon become second nature. For example it is recommended to read Ayat al-Kursi after every *fard salah*;[4] to recite the last two *ayahs* of Surah al-Baqarah,[5] Surah

---

4 Sunan an-Nasa'i
5 Sahih al-Bukhari and Muslim

al-Kafirun[6] and the last three *surah*s of the Qur'an[7] before going to sleep.

❖ Seek forgiveness by reciting *Istighfar*, simply by saying:
Astaghfirullah
I seek forgiveness from Allah.

Reading

It is part of our *deen* to seek and gain knowledge in order to increase our Iman. The most important thing to read and understand, of course, is the Qur'an. But also incorporate Islamic books to gain knowledge, inspire you and motivate you.

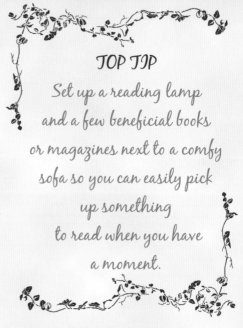

TOP TIP

Set up a reading lamp and a few beneficial books or magazines next to a comfy sofa so you can easily pick up something to read when you have a moment.

Listening

Listening is an ideal portal for busy mums who have no time to sit. Often the mind of the new mother becomes a blur of sleepless nights and countless nappy changes. You may long for someone to talk to or

---

6 Sunan Abu Dawud and Jami' at-Tirmidhi
7 Sahih al-Bukhari

A Gift for the New Muslim Mother

some mental stimulation. It helps to set up a CD player or attach some speakers to your laptop or phone. This way you can listen to Qur'an and religious talks whilst you get on with your daily chores and attend to your baby. This is a very good idea if you feel like you have been pulled away, so to speak. Listening to the Qur'an will be soothing for the heart and calming for the mind and soul, while listening to talks can be both instructive and inspiring.

Du'a

Du'a is a wonderfully personal way of connecting with Allah. You can either use classic *du'a*s from the hadith books or just sit and make *du'a* from your heart for Allah to ease whatever concerns, apprehensions and worries you may have. A good general *du'a* is:

اللَّهُمَّ إِنِّي أَعُوذُ بِكَ مِنَ الهَمِّ وَالحَزَنِ وَالعَجْزِ وَالكَسَلِ وَالبُخْلِ وَالجُبْنِ وَضَلَعِ الدَّيْنِ وَغَلَبَةِ الرِّجَالِ

Allahumma inni a'udhu bika minal hammi walhazani, wal'ajzi, walkasali, walbukhli, waljubni, waldha'id-dayni wa ghalabatir-rijal

O Allah! I seek refuge in You from grief and sadness, from weakness and from laziness, from miserliness and from cowardice, from being overcome by debt and overpowered by others.[8]

8 Sahih al-Bukhari

Now that you are a parent, you have a better understanding of your own parents sacrificed to raise you. A good *du'a* for your parents is:

رَبِّ ارْحَمْهُمَا كَمَا رَبَّيَانِي صَغِيرًا

Rabbir-humhuma kama rabbayani sagheerun

"My Lord! Bestow on them thy mercy even as they cherished me in childhood." (Surah 17:24)

Reading the following *du'a* over small children is a good practice for their protection:

أُعِيذُكُمَا بِكَلِمَاتِ اللّٰهِ التَّامَّةِ مِنْ كُلِّ شَيْطَانٍ وَهَامَّةٍ وَمِنْ كُلِّ عَيْنٍ لَامَّةٍ

U'eedhukuma bikalimatil-lahit-tammati min kulli shaytanin wa hammatin, wa min kulli 'aynin lammatin.

I seek protection for you in the Perfect Words of Allah from every devil and every beast, and from every envious blameworthy eye.[9]

Whichever way you seek to strengthen your connection with Allah, you can be rest assured that your efforts will never go to waste as Allah Himself assures us:

"Remember Me and I will remember you." (Surah 2:152)

---

9 Sahih al-Bukhari

Family Issues

*I*deally, the arrival of a little one is cause for celebration and all the members of the extended family pull together in support. Sometimes, however, not everyone adjusts to the change at the same pace and so issues may arise with your spouse, family, in-laws or friends at this turning point in your life, which you need to be aware of and deal with gracefully.

It may be that you feel your husband is not contributing enough in the care of the baby; perhaps your family or in-laws are not offering you the support you need or have unrealistic expectations that are causing you unnecessary stress.

Ignoring or silently absorbing these pressures is not a healthy way to deal with them in the long term. If you need more help from your husband, you need to gently let him know exactly what you need help with. He can't read your mind and he is also trying to adjust to a major life change. You could also ask for your husband's help in dealing with your in-laws if you are finding it difficult for the time being.

If possible, it is a good idea to have a friend or family member stay with you for a few days after the birth so they can deal with well-meaning but opinionated visitors, field the numerous telephone calls you may be receiving and generally offer support at this most intense time.

TOP TIP

Switch off your phone when you need some space and arrange for visitors to come in groups at certain times.

This will help you settle more quickly into a routine which is better for both you and baby.

If you are feeling overwhelmed by problems and issues, the following is a wonderful *du'a* that will insha'Allah give you the strength and *sabr* to get past the most difficult moments:

حَسْبُنَا اللَّهُ وَنِعْمَ الْوَكِيلُ

Hasbunallahu wa ni'mal wakeel.
Allah suffices is and He is the best guardian.[10]

---

10 Sunan Abu Dawud

Traditions

The birth of a baby is a social event and everyone, in their happiness, will offer you their unsolicited advice and opinions. Do remember that the vast majority of this is well-intentioned and that they are truly happy for you. You may receive some real pearls of wisdom from experienced mothers, but on the same token, you may also hear some suggestions, that are interesting, to say the least, depending on your cultural background. Trust your instinct as to which pieces of advice you wish to take on board and which you do not.

If you are in doubt as to a matter of religion, then consult the Qur'an and hadith. For example, it is commonly thought that a woman is excused from certain religious duties for a fixed period of forty days after childbirth. This is the maximum period of *nifas* (post-partum bleeding). There is no minimum period, so if a woman is free of bleeding after, say, ten days then she can perform ghusl and resume *salah* etc. without waiting for the full forty days to pass.

In some cultures, families can feel disappointed at the birth of a girl and this can have a negative effect on the new mother and her relationship with the baby. If you find yourself within such a family, then there are a wealth of ahadith that highlight the particular rewards for raising daughters that you can find comfort in. A baby is a gift and a trust from Allah that should be treasured unconditionally.

"He bestows (children) male or female according to His will (and plan) or He bestows both males and females, and He leaves barren whom He will…" (Surah 42:49–50)

Whatever the nature of the comments you receive, accept them graciously with a smile and a nod. Have confidence in your abilities as a mother. You are adequate and you can cope with it, which is why Allah blessed you with the honourable task of bringing up this child.

Difficult Circumstances

*W*hatever hardships and difficulties we feel we are facing, we can find an inspirational role model with noble qualities from whom we can gain strength and hope. As women, wives and mothers, our role models should initially be the Prophet ﷺ and women in Islamic history, such as:

Khadijah – the first wife of the Prophet ﷺ

Fatima – the daughter of the Prophet ﷺ

Maryam – the mother of Isa عليه السلام

Asiya – the wife of Pharaoh

Hajar – the wife of Ibrahim عليه السلام

(may Allah be pleased with them all).

Khadija was the mother of six of the Prophet's ﷺ children as well as being a supportive wife to the Prophet ﷺ and a successful and wealthy businesswoman in her own right. Of Khadija, the Prophet ﷺ said: "She believed in me when no-one else did; she accepted Islam when people rejected me; and she helped and comforted me when there was no-one else to lend me a helping hand." SubhanAllah, what an amazing wife!

One of her children was Fatima, who lived her married life in simplicity, carrying out all the domestic chores by herself until she had calluses on her hands. When she asked her father for domestic help, he replied:

"May I point towards something better than you have asked for? When you go to bed, you should recite SubhanAllah *thirty-three times,* Alhamdulillah *thirty-three times and* Allahu Akbar *thirty-four times – and that will be better than a servant for you."*
(Sahih al-Bukhari)

This is a beautiful hadith for us when we feel overwhelmed with responsibilities and feel like we could use a helping hand.

Maryam was the sole parent to Prophet Isa ﷺ, and a beautiful example to those mothers who have the task of bringing up their child as a single parent. She faced her labour alone and even cried out to Allah, **"Oh if only I had died before this time, and were something discarded and forgotten."**[11] She relied on Allah alone, faced her people with dignity even in the face of false allegations and slander and Allah elevated her station with Him and among all of mankind as one of the best of women for eternity.

Asiya, the believing wife of Pharaoh, raised Musa ﷺ and nurtured a close relationship with her Lord despite the hatred and denial of her husband. She was threatened by her husband but she turned to Allah alone crying, **"Oh my Lord! Build for me in nearness to Thee, a mansion in the garden and save me from Pharaoh and his doings, and save me from those that do wrong."**[12] And Allah preserved her faith and raised her status with Him.

And Hajar, the wife of Ibrahim ﷺ, who called out to Allah alone in desperation to save her baby Ismail ﷺ when he was crying of thirst in the middle of the desert. Allah rewarded her and her baby with the water of ZamZam that is still drunk to this day.

---

11 Surah 19:23

12 Surah 66:11

So while there are times we may feel desperate, overwhelmed and as if no one understands, Allah is with us. Turn to Him for support with patience and gratitude and the rewards will, insha'Allah, be unimaginable.

"So verily with every difficulty there is relief.
Verily with every difficulty there is relief."
(Surah 94:5-6)

TOP TIP
Read the Seerah.
It's the most inspiring story
of the most amazing man
ever to walk the face of
the earth.

Final

Words of

Wisdom

Motherhood is a life changing experience that is both challenging and exciting. For all the nights that you will sit up with your baby, for all the trying and tearful times, insha'Allah, you will be rewarded by Allah. An extremely beautiful and powerful story that has always stayed with me was narrated by the Companion of the Prophet Muhammad ﷺ, Abdullah Ibn 'Umar.

A Yemeni man performed tawaf while carrying his mother on his back. This man said to Abdullah ibn 'Umar, *"I am like a tame camel for her! I have carried her more than she carried me. Do you think I have paid her back, O Ibn 'Umar?"* Abdullah Ibn 'Umar replied, *"No, not even for one contraction!"* (Al-Adab al-Mufrad al-Bukhari)

SubhanAllah, the efforts that this man carried out whilst performing *tawaf* was still not enough to repay his mother for a single contraction she experienced through childbirth to have him.

The prestigious status of motherhood has been somewhat lowered in the modern age that gives more importance to careers and earning potential. Being a mother is looked upon as something to postpone until you have reached a certain point in your career. But this statement of Abdullah ibn 'Umar's clearly shows the tremendous value and prestigious position a mother has always held in Islam.

The love and mercy we feel towards our child is also a reminder of the greater love and mercy Allah bestows upon us and His tending to our every need, whether or not we are aware of Him.

Narrated from Abu Hurayrah that the Prophet ﷺ said, *"Allah has one hundred parts of mercy, of which He sent down one between the jinn, mankind, the animals and the insects, by means of which they are compassionate and merciful to one another, and by means of which wild animals are kind to their offspring. And Allah has kept back ninety-nine parts of mercy with which to be merciful to His slaves of the Day of Resurrection."* (Sahih Muslim)

Insha'Allah every time you look at your baby, you will be filled with hope and faith that this is the best job in the world and that Allah has bestowed on you an important and great task that, by His Will, you can certainly fulfil.

There are no words that can describe the feeling of being a mother other than the fact that motherhood is truly amazing. . .

Recommended Texts And Reading

Interpretation of the Meanings of The Noble Quran (In the English Language, Summarized in One Volume)
Dr Muhammad Muhsin Khan,
Dr Muhammad Taqi-ud-Din Al Hilali
(Darussalam, 1996)

The Translation of the Meanings of Sahih Al-Bukhari (Arabic-English)
Dr. Muhammad Muhsin Khan
(Darussalam, 1997)

Fortress Of the Muslim
Abdul Malik Mujahid
(Darussalam Research Division, 2003)

The Life of Muhammad ﷺ
Tahia Ismail
(Ta-Ha Publishers Ltd., 2006)

The Life of Muhammad ﷺ from the earliest sources
Martin Lings
(ITS, 1991)

Muhammad ﷺ: Man and Conduct
Adil Salahi
(The Islamic Foundation, 2013)

The Wives of the Prophet
Muhammad ﷺ
Ahmad Thomson
(Ta-Ha Publishers Ltd., 2012)

The Muslim Parent's Guide to the
Early Years 0-5 years
Umm Safiyyah bint Najmuddin
(Ta-Ha Publishers Ltd., 2011)

Cherishing Childhood
Dr. Abdul Bari
(Ta-Ha Publishers Ltd., 2015)

Patience and Gratitude
Ibn Taymiyyah
(Ta-Ha Publishers Ltd., 2007)

In the Early Hours
Khurram Murad
(The Islamic Foundation, 2008)